THE PEAK DISTRICT .....something to remember her by.

by JOHN N. MERRILL

a J.N.M. PUBLICATION

JNM PUBLICATIONS,
WINSTER,
MATLOCK,
DERBYSHIRE.
ENGLAND.
DE4 2DQ

Conceived, edited, typeset, designed, marketed and distributed by John N. Merrill.

© Text — John N. Merrill 1987

© Maps and photographs — John N. Merrill 1987

First Published — October 1987

ISBN 0 907496 53 9

Meticulous research has been undertaken to ensure that this publication is highly accurate at the time of going to press. The publishers, however, cannot be held responsible for alterations, errors or omissions, but they would welcome notification of such for future editions.

Set in Baskerville — Roman and Bold.
Printed and bound in England by
Netherwood Dalton & Co. Ltd., Huddersfield

CONTENTS

INTRODUCTION

The Peak District National Park is a remarkably scenic area extremely broad in its variety, with gritstone moorlands and edges, and limestone dales and plateaus. Here, in a space of a few miles, you can walk over peat moorland startling red grouse, along the top of sixty foot high gritstone edges, before descending to a river and walking along the floor of a limestone dale. The Park is a walker's paradise with such character compressed into a small area. The only way to learn, understand and discover the Peak Park, is on foot. What makes the area even more enjoyable to explore is its tremendous wealth of villages with fascinating churches, old customs, impressive Halls and remains of former industries.

Over the last twenty years I have spent most of my time learning about the area by walking more than 30,000 miles. I never get tired of walking the same paths many times, for the different seasons bring different views and outlooks. The joy of walking out in early spring seeing the countryside awake from winter's sleep and the early flowers pushing their way through; the birds busy building their nests; and the trees dramatically and suddenly opening their new leaves, are moments not to be forgotten. Winter, although a drab landscape until covered with snow and icicles, is a period of peace when the land sleeps and only the hardy walkers are out. The early summer sees the ground carpeted with flowers and the countryside alive with new colours and smells. Autumn lasts all too briefly and only for a handful of days do the trees expose their autumn gold. But, it is a magical time with the scenes of vivid colours which you never forget.

I began walking and climbing for physical exercise and challenge. But I have an enquiring mind which led me from pushing my body hard up the peaks to wanting to learn the story behind a place name on the map, or who built that Hall, or what is the legend behind that stone. As a result I began to spend just as much time researching as walking. Then, inevitably I began to wonder how to make a living and began to write about what I was discovering. The result is that I am one of those fortunate people whose hobby is also one's "job". This book is therefore a continuation of my work.

When I first began putting my ideas together for this book, I hadn't realised what a task I had set myself. At first I planned to include both the Peak District and Derbyshire, but soon realised the scope was too vast. I then concentrated on the Peak District and including key places like Matlock, Buxton and Ashbourne which lie outside the National Park boundary. But again the task was too big. In the end I became ruthless and decided I had to keep within the Park's boundary. The next stage was choosing which colour photographs to use. For three months I viewed my 6,000 Peak District collection, slowly editing my selection; again I had to be ruthless, often discarding some of my favourite shots for the sake of getting an even coverage.

My final choice has been hard to arrive at but I have endeavoured to get an overall coverage of the many facets that make up the Peak District National Park. Some of the views are almost obligatory but I have attempted to cover all aspects, often with views from different angles and different seasons. I can only hope the result is a fair one photographically recording a unique slice of England's scenery and for those who visit or live in the area .... something to remember her by.

HAPPY WALKING!

JOHN N. MERRILL
WINSTER. JULY 1987

2

GRITSTONE MOORLAND COUNTRY

North of the Edale Valley and covering almost a third of the National Park are the gritstone moors of the "High Peak". Here the moorland attains a height of just over 2,000 feet, the highest point in the Park. It is a bleak landscape crossed by few roads, covered by peat, bilberry, crowberry, cotton grass and heather. In fine weather it is a remote walking area, but in mist and rain becomes a serious undertaking with boggy ground and little shelter. Crossing the area is the Pennine Way, via Kinder, Bleaklow and Black Hill. Red Grouse abound with snipe and curlew often seen. It is still a popular shooting area and from the "Glorious Twelth" many of the moors are closed for a day's shoot. Outside these closures it is "open country" to be explored and enjoyed.

The northern end is dominated by the scenic Chew Valley and the bleak and aptly named Black Hill. Dividing the area is Longdendale with Bleaklow to the south, where the infant River Derwent begins its 66 mile journey to the River Trent via the Derwent Valley and the three reservoirs of Howden, Derwent and Ladybower. Dividing this mass is the Snake Road, with Kinder at the southern end of the area, whose plateau's perimeter has gritstone outcrops and the impressive Kinder Downfall. Old packhorse routes lead via Edale and Edale Cross to Hayfield, and an old Roman Road links the Roman Forts of Melandra (Glossop) with Navio, near Brough in the Hope Valley.

The top of Grindsbrook on the southern edge of Kinder Scout.

Chew Valley with Dove Stone Reservoir in the distance. Taken from near Chew Reservoir.

Laddow Rocks and Crowden Great Brook with the Pennine Way path clearly visible. The rocks have several fine climbs and are one of the earliest climbing areas in the Peak District.

Close to the source of the River Derwent, taken from the slopes of Barrow Stones on the Howden Moors, looking down on the infant river. The path beside it leads down to Slippery Stones and Howden Reservoir.

6

Slippery Stones, upper Derwent valley beneath the slopes of Margery Hill. The packhorse bridge over the River Derwent was moved here from Derwent village, before the village was submerged by Ladybower Reservoir in the 1940's.

Alport Dale from near Hope Cross. The eastern side of the dale is dominated by Alport Castles, a huge landslip. At Alport Castle Farm is held in early July a "love feast", a religious service by the Methodists dating back to the 17th century.

The partially revealed Roman Road at Doctor's Gate, near the summit of the Snake Pass. The road linked the Roman forts at Melandra (Glossop) with Navio near Brough in the Hope Valley.

Mermaid's Pool with Kinder Reservoir in the distance. The pool lies below Kinder Downfall. It is said that if you visit the pool early on Easter Sunday morning and see the mermaid, you will gain everlasting life. No one has admitted to seeing her, but Aaron Ashton of Hayfield came regularly and died in 1835 aged 104.

Kinder Downfall in summer.

Kinder Downfall in winter, making an excellent 120 foot ice climb.

Grindsbrook, the upper half through which the Pennine Way ascends to the Kinder Plateau.

Grindsbrook in winter. Wintertime is often the best time to walk on the northern moorlands when the peat surface is frozen giving firm and dry footing. It is also a time when the frozen brooks and cloughs give the added excitement of scrambling up the frozen falls.

Looking down onto the Grindsbook path from Nether Tor, with the Edale Valley and Mam Tor in the distance.

Derwent Reservoir wall. Completed in 1916, the reservoir has a holding capacity of 2,220 million gallons. Howden Reservoir, the upper reservoir, was built in 1912 and has a holding capacity of 1,980 million gallons. The lower reservoir, Ladybower, was completed in 1945.

Crook Hill and Ladybower Reservoir in Autumn from the lower slopes of Win Hill.

Ladybower Reservoir and Ashopton viaduct with Bamford Edge in the distance, one winter's afternoon. Building of Ladybower Reservoir in the 1940's meant the evacuation and demolishment of two villages, Derwent and Ashopton. The viaduct stands 150 feet above the village site. The reservoir has a holding capacity of 6,310 million gallons.

The Peakland Ridge, the dividing line of the gritstone and limestone country. Taken from Mam Tor looking along the ridge to Back Tor and Lose Hill with Win Hill in the background. The finest ridge walk in the Peak District.

Mam Tor's eastern face one January morning. Often referred to as the Shivering Mountain because of its loose layers of grit and shale. The road beneath it has been abandoned due to considerable subsidence. The summit provides an exceptional vantage point over Kinder and the Hope Valley. A seven foot deep ditch encircles the summit — about 1,200 yards long — and is the remains of an Iron Age fort, the largest in Derbyshire.

Back Tor and its northern face from Hollins Cross, the main crossing point on the ridge between Edale and Castleton. It was along this path that the dead were taken from Edale to be buried in Castleton.

Lose Hill in Autumn. It is said that this hill and Win Hill opposite are named after a battle here in 626 A.D. between the Kings of Wessex and Northumberland. The winners — Edwin, King of Northumberland — camped on Win Hill. The River Noe which flows between them was said to have turned red during the battle.

The Vale of Edale from the slopes of Win Hill.

The road at Yorkshire Bridge at the base of Win Hill in autumn. From here a steep path leads to the summit. The bridge is on the site of a wooden bridge and a stone one was built in 1695. The crossing of the River Derwent at this point was on an important packhorse route from Hope Cross to Stanage Edge and onto Sheffield.

Map showing locations: HUDDERSFIELD, MANCHESTER, GLOSSOP, ERRWOOD RESERVOIR, KETTLESHULME, WINDGATHER ROCKS, MACCLESFIELD, SHEFFIELD, DERWENT STEPPING STONES, STANAGE EDGE, HATHERSAGE, HIGGER TOR, SURPRISE VIEW, LAWRENCEFIELD, PADLEY GORGE, FROGGATT EDGE, GARDOMS EDGE, BASLOW EDGE, BUXTON, CHESTERFIELD, THREE SHIRE HEADS, ROBIN HOOD'S STRIDE, CRATCLIFFE TOR, MATLOCK, LEEK, PHOTO LOCATIONS, ASHBOURNE

GRITSTONE EDGE COUNTRY

In cross section the Peak District, geologically, is saucer-shaped with gritstone edges on the eastern and western perimeters with limestone in the middle. The limestone is often referred to as the Derbyshire Dome. Millions of years ago underground movement pushed the limestone upwards cracking the gritstone, which in time eroded away leaving the edges as a prominent feature. The edges are popular walking terrain, either along their tops or beneath them. The edges, which rise up to eighty feet high and as long as four miles, played an important part in the development of rock climbing as a sport. Today there are thousands of routes of varying difficulty up the coarse rock.

Beneath many of the edges can be found remains of local millstone industry with abandoned and faulty millstones lying around. The industry ceased in the mid 19th century. Below the edges on the eastern side flows the River Derwent, beside which many mills operated grinding corn and further down cotton spinning mills. The gritstone villages are full of character and well worth exploring in their own right, as can be seen in the customs and churches sections. The western side has equally impressive edges including Windgather Rocks above the Goyt Valley. To the south lies Ramshaw Rocks and The Roaches.

Froggatt Pinnacle, a popular climbing route just off Froggatt Edge, standing 55 feet high and approximately 20 feet square.

23

Stepping Stones across the River Derwent, ½ mile west of Hathersage. The paths take you beside the river to Grindleford and Shatton or up to Offerton Hall and Moor.

Hathersage, famed for its needle manufacturing last century, is now best remembered as the resting place of Robin Hood's faithful friend, Little John. His grave is in the churchyard and he was said to be seven feet tall. The church has brasses to the Eyre family who onced owned most of the Hope Valley and had seven Halls including North Lees and Moorseats, where Charlotte Bronte stayed and is immortalised in her book,"Jane Eyre".

Stanage Edge, the longest gritstone edge, almost four miles long and now a rock climbers' haven with more than 700 different routes.

Surprise View. One of the most stunning views in the Peak District as you drive round the corner close to Millstone Edge.

The view lies up the Hope Valley to Win Hill and Mam Tor.

Abandoned millstones beneath Surprise View. The millstone industry lasted 500 years until the latter half of last century. In 1862 rollers began to be used and the millstone industry ceased quickly and accounts for many of the abandoned and stacked stones lying around today. In 1811 a 5 ft diameter millstone was sold for 10 guineas (£10.50).

Lawrencefield, beneath Surprise View and a popular climbing ground.

The Eagle Stone above Baslow Edge. Before a local person could be married it was obligatory that he should show his worthiness by ascending the stone. If he didn't, no marriage!

Higger Tor on the western side of the Burbage Valley. The large leaning block on the lefthand side of the photograph is 45 feet high and overhangs 15 feet. ½ mile to the south is Carl Wark, an Iron Age fort occupying a small rocky plateau with natural defences and a man made ten foot high wall on its western end.

Padley Gorge. A delightful walk through a rocky tree-covered gorge from Longshaw to Grindleford Station. Close by is the 14th century Padley Chapel and remains of Padley Manor. The chapel's stained glass windows depict its tragic history resulting in the hung, drawn and quartering of three Roman Catholic priests in Derby in 1588. An annual pilgrimage to the Padley Martyrs take place here in July.

Froggatt Edge, one of the most picturesque edges whose footpath is above it providing distant views into central Peakland.

Froggatt village nestling beside the River Derwent below Froggatt Edge.

View from Froggatt Edge to Curbar and central Peak District.

Rainbow over Wellington's Monument on Baslow Edge with Gardoms Edge in the background. The monument records the visit by the Duke of Wellington, the Iron Duke, who died in 1852. Beyond Gardoms Edge is Birchens Edge, upon which is

Nelson's Monument erected in 1810 by John Brightman of Baslow. Nearby three large shiplike boulders bear the names Victory, Defiant and Royal.

Gardoms Edge with Birchens Edge beyond.

Cratcliffe Tor, near Birchover. At the base of the rocks behind a wrought iron fence is a hermit's cave dating back to the 14th century. A carved crucifix and shelves can be seen.

Robin Hood's Stride, near Birchover. Often referred to as Mock Beggar's Hall, for from afar the twin pinnacles look like chimneys. The rocks are named after Robin Hood and the distance between the pinnacles is said to be the length of his stride!

Windgather Rocks above the Goyt Valley and one of the earliest edges to be climbed.

Kettleshulme from near Reed Hill with Windgather Rocks on the righthand skyline.

Errwood Reservoir in the Goyt Valley. When Fernilee Reservoir was built in 1938 Errwood Hall was pulled down, although its ruins still remain today surrounded by thousands of rhododendrons. Errwood Reservoir was built in 1967 and the valley is one of the most popular areas on the western side of the National Park.

Three Shire Heads near Flash in the Dane Valley. As the name implies, the counties of Cheshire, Derbyshire and Staffordshire meet here. The river is crossed by packhorse bridges and several packhorse routes radiate out from here. One of the pools is aptly named, Panniers Pool.

In the south is the well known River Dove and her dale system, whose beauty is second to none. Just to the west in direct contrast is the Manifold Valley, much more open with limestone cliffs and a dissappearing river. The limestone plateau is traversed by three old railway lines now transformed to leisureways and known as the High Peak Trail, Tissington Trail, and Monsal Trail. The villages continue the unique Derbyshire custom of well dressing, and the summer programme is full of local shows, fairs and wakes.

Lathkill Dale near the junction with Cales Dale.

LIMESTONE DALE COUNTRY

Starting from Castleton in the north the limestone country broadens out and encompasses some of the finest scenery in England. The landscape is softer than its gritstone counterpart, with gentle sided dales, crystal clear flowing rivers and lusher foliage. The walking is gentler too through the dales to attractive villages and their churches, inns and halls. There are more than a hundred dales; some like Monsal Dale and Lathkill are well known, but others such as Woo Dale and Long Dale are known only to the few. Wild flowers grow in abundance and a wide variety of birds are sighted in the dales and plateaux.

Deep Dale near Buxton with prominent cave in upper centre of the photograph, said to be the home of Hob Hirst. The cave is approximately seventy feet long.

Foolow Village Green and Pond. The cross dates from the 14th century and was placed here in 1868. Beside it is a bull ring, one of only five in the county. Bull baiting was one of the highlights of Wakes week in the 18th century but its practice was abolished in the mid 19th century.

View down onto the limestone village of Bradwell from the gritstone country of Bradwell Edge. In the distance can be seen the chimney of the Hope Cement works and on the skyline the Kinder plateau.

Avenue of beech trees close to the entrance to Tideswell Dale. The dale has a nature trail and a small basalt quarry with splendid examples of spherodical weathering.

Water Cum Jolly Dale and River Wye, between Litton and Cressbrook.

Monsal Dale Viaduct now part of the Monsal Trail and standing 120 feet above the River Wye.

Monsal Dale Weir.

Sheepwash Bridge, Ashford in the Water. The bridge dates from the 17th century and was used for washing sheep until a few years ago; the sheep pen can be seen on the lefthand side.

The River Wye at Bakewell and Scot's meadows.

Lathkill Dale in winter near the junction with Cales Dale.

The River Lathkill in full flood in Lathkill Dale near the village of Alport.

View of Youlgreave from the west with moorland of Stanton Moor and Brampton Moor in the distance.

Classic Peak District buildings in the square at Middleton by Youlgreave, dating from the early 19th century.

Wolfscote Dale and the River Dove at the junction with Biggin Dale.

The River Dove and Ravens Tor near Milldale.

Thorpe Cloud at the southern end of Dove Dale. The brief ascent of the 942 foot high hill provides a stunning viewpoint down onto the dale and the flatter country to the south outside the National Park.

The River Dove south of the stepping stones beneath the slopes of Thorpe Cloud.

Thor's Cave in the Manifold Valley near Wetton. The cave is reached by paths from Wetton and the valley floor has been excavated — finds are on display in Derby museum. The finds reveal that the cave was occupied by prehistoric man. Running along the valley floor was the Leek and Manifold Light Railway which ceased operating in 1934. The track has been removed and is now a delightful walk and cycleway through a deep valley from Hulme End in the north to Waterhouses in the south.

Tunnel near Friden on the High Peak Trail. The trail is a former railway line which linked the Cromford Canal with the Peak Forest Canal at Whaley Bridge. The line was 30 miles long with nine inclines. The journey took two days, and although it cost £180,000 to build was never a profitable line. In 1972 a major section was opened to the public as a walkway, cycle and horse riding route. The stations were converted to car parks. The nearby Tissington Trail which the High Peak Trail joins near Hartington is a similar conversion of 13 miles to Ashbourne and was opened in 1971.

Many are universally known, such as Chatsworth House and Haddon Hall, but I have endeavoured to encompass a broad section of what is to be seen, including Peveril Castle, the only castle in the Peak District. On the limestone plateau is Minninglow, a prehistoric burial chamber. A little to the north is Arbor Low, the "Stonehenge of the Peak". Lesser known Halls such as Parwich and Castern are included, and classic examples of their type. With more than 300 Halls and manor houses there is plenty of scope!

Hazlebadge Hall, one mile south of Bradwell. Built in 1549 as one of the manors of the Vernons of Haddon Hall. The Vernon coat of arms can be seen above the upper mullioned window.

HISTORICAL BUILDINGS & ANCIENT MONUMENTS

The Peak District contains a remarkably diverse range of buildings and monuments, from the Stone Age to some of the finest buildings of England from medieval times and 18th century splendour. In the northern moors are Roman forts and roads. A little to the south are Iron Age forts occupying lofty locations, while in the valleys majestic Halls of the Lords of the Manor and gentry add grandeur to an already incomparable setting. This is what makes exploring the area so fascinating, seeing at first hand the work of local families through generations creating today's scene.

63

Lyme Hall — south front. The Legh family lived on the estate for 600 years until Richard Legh, the third Lord Newton, gave the house and its 1,323 acres of parkland together with its herd of red deer to the National Trust. The Hall contains an Elizabethan Long Gallery built in 1541 but much of the present Palladian building dates from the 18th century.

The Norman Keep, Peveril Castle. Formerly known as the Castle of the Peak. The Castle, overlooking Castleton, dates from the 11th century. The Keep was built in 1176 and cost £135. Despite its location no battle took place and from early 1400 it was little used.

Longshaw Lodge, on the edge of the City of Sheffield. Former shooting lodge of the Dukes of Rutland (Haddon Hall), who constructed the many drives through the estate. It is now a National Trust country park. The Longshaw sheep dog trials in early September take place in the field in front of the lodge.

Chatsworth House from the Elizabethan Shooting Lodge. From here you can appreciate the perfect setting of the building in delightful parkland bordering the River Derwent.

Chatsworth House from the archway of the Paine bridge, built in 1761. The house, the home of the Dukes of Devonshire, took almost 200 years to complete today's setting. The west front, in the photograph, was built between 1699-1702. The sixth Duke together with his gardener Sir Joseph Paxton in the mid 19th century finalised the building and gardens. The house stands on the site of an Elizabethan building, part of which is incorporated in today's buildings, and was built by the redoubtable Bess of Hardwick at a cost of £80,000.

Eyam Hall, built by the Wright family in 1676. The stone came from Bradshaw Hall, part of which still stands today near Eyam car park.

Bakewell Old Town Hall, built in 1602 as the Town Hall and Courtroom. Later the building served as a library, a fire station and in 1964 a chip shop! Thankfully it has been restored. The square outside was a butter market, and the stocks would have been located here.

Haddon Hall from Haddon Fields. The finest manorial home in England. The building spans 350 years and remains little altered from the mid 16th century. The Vernon family were the main builders with Sir George Vernon, known as the King of the Peak, as the last in the male line. His daughter, Dorothy Vernon, whose love story is forever entwined with the building, married Sir John Manners who later became the Duke of Rutland. Descendants of this family own it today.

Haddon Hall, south front from the rose garden showing the Long Gallery. This was the last part to be built in the mid 16th century. The hall was little used from 1700 onwards as the Duke of Rutland was engaged in building Belvoir Castle. It was left to a later Duke this century who restored and preserved this wonderful building.

Winster Market Hall. The village of Winster deseves a second look and is full of impressive buildings from the 17th century, resulting from the profitable lead mines nearby. The Market House dates from the 16th century, and originally the lower arches would have been open. The upper half is 18th century replacing an earlier wooden construction. In 1906 it was given to the National Trust who restored it at a cost of £165. It was their first property in Derbyshire.

Arbor Low, two miles south of Monyash, and often referred to as the "Stonehenge of the Peak". Dates from the Bronze Age (2,000 B.C.) with ditch and circle of 46 stones. It is a point of conjecture whether they ever stood upright as at Stonehenge.

Minninglow, west of Grangemill and close to the High Peak Trail. Just beside it is the line of a Roman road which ran between Derby and Buxton. The "low" has five burial chambers formed by limestone boulders and date from the Bronze Age. The hill is topped by a cluster of windswept trees which make a useful landmark for the area.

Tissington Hall dates from 1609 and was built by Francis Fitzherbert. The Fitzherberts, a leading Derbyshire family, still reside here today. The library wing was added in 1910 and the stable clock was made in Ashbourne in the mid 18th century. Monuments to the Fitzherberts can be seen in Tissington church.

Parwich Hall was built in 1747 by Sir Richard Levinge and is faced with red brick at the front. The rear is limestone from the earlier building.

Alsop en le Dale Hall, is a delightful twin gabled 17th century Hall tucked away near Parwich in the southern end of the Park.

Castern Hall, near Ilam in the Manifold Valley, dates from the 18th century and is the home of the Hurt family who have resided here for 400 years.

CUSTOMS

During the summer months every week a different village "dresses" its wells in the unique and extremely colourful custom of well-dressing, whose origins date back to the 14th century. In Castleton in late May the "Garland Ceremony" takes place, and in July at Alport a religious "Love Feast" is held. In August Eyam, renowned for its 17th century plague, holds a commemorative service and well dressing. In many villages local and visiting Morris Men dance their dances, of which Winster's team is well respected. The village also holds Pancake Races on Shrove Tuesday. To complete the survey the old sad Midland custom of funeral garlands is recorded. Interlaced with these customs are numerous fairs, wakes weeks, local shows and sheep dog trials; a full programme.

Tissington Well Dressing — Town Well.

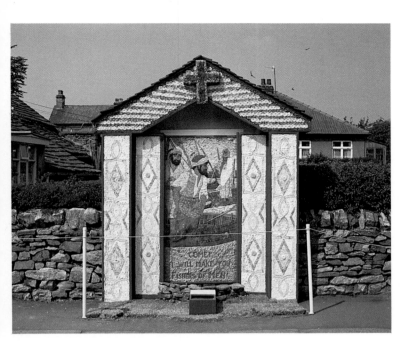

Hope Well Dressing — complete well.

There are now three wells dressed in late June, although when they began, in 1949, just the Edale Road Well was dressed.

Hope Well Dressing — central feature.

Monyash Well Dressing. The village has about twenty wells, but it was not until 1974 that it first dressed a well.

These colour mosaics of flowers depict a biblical or topical theme. The wooden base is lined with well puddled clay before the time consuming task of placing thousands of flower petals and pieces of foliage to create the picture. The result is a stunning display and remains in place for a week following its blessing ceremony.

As an indication of the work involved to create a well-dressing, one well involved —
65 helpers working 421 hours — checking 2750 nails on the frame, puddling ¼ ton of clay, adding ten cups of salt to the clay, fitting in 10,010 petals, 10994 bits of corn, 665 alder cones, 450 spruce tips, 5lbs of seed, 2 buckets of moss, 1 bucket of parsley and spurge, 1 bucket of rhubarb seed, and 1 bucket of leaves. During the work they consumed 198 cups of coffee and ate one barrowfull of fish and chips!

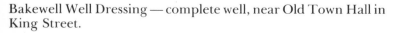

Bakewell Well Dressing — complete well, near Old Town Hall in King Street.

Bakewell dresses its wells in late June/early July, and they started in 1971. Two other wells are dressed in Bath Gardens.

Bakewell Well Dressing — central mosaic.

Tissington is known as the "Mother of Well Dressing" and has been dressing its five wells for several centuries. The origin of well dressing is believed to have begun here in 1350. During the Black Death, 1348-9, many Derbyshire priests died, because of contaminated water. The five wells at Tissington remained pure and no one died. As an offering to give thanks for their survival the wells were dressed annually, although in later years the custom lapsed. It was revived again in 1950, and now more and more villages, several outside the Peak District, annually dress their wells.

The Hands Well, Tissington.

Eyam Plague Cottage.

Thomas Mosley plaque.

Sydall family plaque.

In 1665 a tailor, George Vicars, who lived in the now named Plague Cottages, received contaminated cloth from London. He died a few days later in September 1665. From then until October 1666 263 people out of a population of 350 died from the disease. The village's struggle, with the help of their Rector, William Mompesson, is one of the tragic stories of the Peak District. Outside many of the houses can be seen the plaques recording who died there and when. In the surrounding area is Mompesson's Well, the Riley Graves, a solitary tomb to Humphrey Merrill (no relation!), and the Cucklet Delf where open-air services were held during this time. The church contains relics of the time and an inscribed list of those who suffered.

Winster Morris Dancers are the sole surviving one in Derbyshire and whose traditions are unique. Their origins date back to the early 19th century, but documented evidence only dates from 1908. Instead of the usual six dancers Winster has sixteen, with four characters and a musician. The characters are all men who dress up as King, Queen, Jester and Witch. In olden days Morris Dancing was one of the highlights of Wakes week — late June in Winster's case — and Winster has five of their own — the Processional, the Blue-eyed Stranger, the Reel, the Morris, and the Gallop. The team flourishes today and can be seen performing in parts of the area and further afield.

Winster Pancake Races. The origin of the races in Winster are unknown, but they have been a feature on the village calendar every Shrove Tuseday for more than 100 years. The races take place down the Main Street and are of various distances depending on age. Special frying pans are used, and the pancakes are made to a special recipe to ensure robustness from the handling they receive. They are not intended to be eaten and, as the participants run, the pancake must be tossed at least three times.

Funeral Garlands in Ilam Church. In the 18th Century it was a popular custom to make a funeral garland to a woman who died before her marriage. The garland in the shape of a birdcage and made from a thin wooden frame and covered in paper flowers and rosettes, with a paper glove or hankerchief hanging down inside with the deceased's name on, was carried at the funeral procession and afterwards hung above the deceased person's pew. Fine examples can seen in Ilam and Ashford in the Water churches and outside the National Park in Matlock and South Trusley churches in Derbyshire.

CHURCHES

The village church is very much an open book on the village and immediate area. Through the gravestones, monuments and plaques you can trace the growth and history of the village. Many of the Peak District churches date from Norman times, with considerable rebuilding and enlarging between 1300-1600. Many of the buildings are classic examples of their period, with Tideswell the most complete 14th century church in England; Youlgreave a magnificent 15th century perpendicular tower; Longnor an elegant classical building; and Stoney Middleton a surprisingly beautiful octagonal shape. The handful shown are a mere taste of what the Peak District has to offer.

Tideswell Church, dedicated to St. John the Baptist, originates from the 12th century, but the present building was started in 1340 and completed by the end of that century. Since then it has been little altered and is the most complete 14th century church in England. Inside are several brasses and tombs to Sir Sampson Meverill who died in 1462, Bishop Pursglove and John Foljambe.

Youlgreave Church, dedicated to All Saints, dates from Norman times. The tower is 15th century and arguably the finest in the Peak District. The font is unusual as it incorporates a Holy Water stoup. Inside the wooden ceilings of the nave and chancel are particularly fine. An altar tomb to Thomas Cockayne who died in 1488 and a monument slab to Robert Gilbert who died in 1492 are both impressive monuments.

Longnor Church is classical in style and was built in 1780. From the outside it appears two storeyed but inside the upper windows are hidden by the false roof. Amongst the gravestones is one to a local blacksmith, and another to William Billinge who died on January 25th 1791, aged 112.

Stoney Middleton Church, dedicated to St. Martin, has a 15th Century perpendicular tower and an octagonal nave built in 1759. The clock came from Baslow church when the latter had its lettered clock — Victoria 1897 — fitted.

Beeley Church, close to Chatsworth Park, has a Norman doorway and a 14th century tower but was mostly rebuilt in 1884. Inside are monuments to the Cavendish family, but their principal graveyard is at nearby Edensor church. Preserved is a basson which was used to accompany the hymns before an organ was fitted.

Eyam Church, dedicated to St. Lawrence, has Norman origins but was mostly rebuilt in 1350. Inside are many monuments and relics associated with the plague — 1665-1666. These include Mompesson's chair, the plague cupboard made from the wooden box in which the contaminated cloth was shipped from London, and the Plague Register. The font is believed to be Saxon, and outside the 8th century Celtic cross is one of the finest in England. Close by is the grave to Catherine Mompesson and another to the Rev. Thomas Stanley; both of whom played a key role during the plague.

Taddington Church is mostly 14th century and contains a magnificent 16th century brass to the Blackwell family, showing their five daughters and six sons. Their home was at the nearby village of Blackwell.

Baslow Church, dedicated to St. Ann, has a 13th century broach spire. On the walls is a square clock with Roman numerals and dated 1759. The other is circular and instead of numbers has — VICTORIA 1897 — and was made by John Smith of Derby. Of particular note inside in a glass case is a dog whip. This is one of the few surviving examples in the country today. In the 17th and 18th century there was an official dog whipper, whose duty was to control the canine foes before and during the service. There was one at Youlgreave and in 1609 — "To Robert Walton for whipping y dogges forth of y church in tyme of divine service... one shilling and four pence". (6p)

Ilam Church, dedicated to the Holy Cross, has a Saxon font and two Saxon cross shafts in the churchyard. Inside are funeral garlands and a tomb to St. Bertram. Of particular note is the Chantry chapel with the beautiful carving by Sir Francis Chantry of the reclining figure of David Pike Watts and his daughter and children. The Watts family were largely responsible for Ilam Hall, now a Youth Hostel and National Trust country park.

Tissington Church, dedicated to St. Mary, has a Norman tower and tympanum and font. Inside are monuments to the Fitzherbert family and several exceptionally attractive stained-glass windows.

WILD FLOWERS

With the wide variety of soil and terrain in the National Park there are literally hundreds of different species of wild flowers. The few I have chosen to illustrate are some of my favourite ones; several are well known while others are rare. All have been taken on my walks and I cannot think of anything finer than to walk through a wood carpeted with wood anemones or along a limestone road fringed with meadow cranesbill. In early summer one sees fields full of cowslips or a quiet dale side clothed in orchids. In late summer the moorland dramatically changes colour as the heather blossoms, giving a purple hue. But this is what walking and exploring the Peak District is all about — you never know what lies just around the corner.

Canterbury Bell, near River Dove, Thorpe.

Cotton Grass, Bleaklow.

Jacob's Ladder, Wolfscote Dale.

Peacock Butterfly and Blackthorn, Ravensdale.

Meadow Cranesbill, Monyash.

Bloody Cranesbill, Deep Dale.

Ransoms, Wood Garlick, Manifold Valley.

Marsh Marigold, Lathkill Dale.

Harebells, Robin Hood's Stride.

Lesser Celandine, Lathkill Dale.

Early Purple Orchid, Deep Dale.

Monkey Flower, Manifold Valley.